PET OWNER'S GUIDE TO THE
COCKER SPANIEL

Frank Kane

RINGPRESS

ABOUT THE AUTHOR

Photo: John Hartley.

Frank Kane is one of the UK's leading all-rounder judges, approved to award Kennel Club Challenge Certificates in some forty breeds. He is approved to judge Best in Show at Championship level as well as the Gundog and Utility groups.

Frank owned his first Cocker Spaniel, a blue roan, in 1961, while a schoolboy. He began exhibiting soon after. He has been involved with Cocker Spaniels ever since. Frank has travelled extensively and judged worldwide. He is a regular contributor to the canine press.

PHOTOGRAPHY: STEPH HOLBROOK

Published by Ringpress Books Limited,
PO Box 8, Lydney, Gloucestershire,
GL15 6YD, United Kingdom.

First published 1999
©1999 Ringpress Books Limited. All rights reserved

ISBN 1 86054 039 2
Printed in Hong Kong through Printworks Int. Ltd.

CONTENTS

1

A Breed History

All the sporting Spaniel breeds we know today are members of the same family, and their ancestry can be traced back to the same roots. The word 'spaniel' gives away the Spanish origins of the breeds, and they were used primarily as sporting dogs to help in the hunting of game – firstly with the falcon, and then with the gun.

In the middle of the 19th century, all of the sporting Spaniels were referred to generally as Field Spaniels, with a weight limit of 25lbs being used to divide the category into Cockers (under 25lbs) and Field Spaniels (over 25lbs). In the earliest dog shows, littermates were often shown in the different categories, depending on their size and weight. At the same time, the leggier Springer Spaniels were being established, with the Sussex Spaniel and Clumber Spaniel also beginning to take definition. This was helped by

the formation of the Spaniel Club in 1885, which drew up breed 'Standards', which meant that breeders could breed for a specific type of dog and help to stabilise the type.

One interesting family feature which was shared by all Spaniel breeds was the docked tail. The tails were docked (that is, cut shorter a few days after birth) because of the function of the breeds – working in thick undergrowth in the hunt for game. The happy working temperament of the Spaniel produced an incessantly wagging tail, which, if left undocked, often resulted in damaged, fractured and bleeding tails. So, docking was not merely a whim of fashion, but also a functional feature, and hence a feature of Spaniel type.

THE COCKER SPANIEL
The Cocker Spaniel acquired its name from the purpose for which

it was originally used – the flushing out of woodcock from coverts and woodland. We can look back to around 1880 for the forefather of the modern Cocker Spaniel – principally, the black dog Obo. In the show ring, Obo was unbeaten, and he was widely used as a sire.

Although black was the dominant colour in the ring, Obo was mated with bitches of all the Spaniel colours, and was influential in producing both solid and particoloured Cockers. Obo can claim to be the tap source of the Cocker Spaniel of today. Mr Farrow, his owner, was a founder member of the Cocker Spaniel Club in 1902. Other early influences on the breed were Mr Phillips and his Rivington Kennel, who used the Obo blood closely to produce both solids and particolours; Mr Richard Lloyd of Ware in Hertfordshire, father of Mr H. S. Lloyd, whose name and 'of Ware' affix became a household name in the Cocker world.

Mr Porter's Braeside particolours combined with the Rivington bloodlines to help establish the particolours, in particular. The Bowdler Kennel of

The merry, sporting Cocker Spaniel soon became a firm favourite in the show ring.

Mr Peele was influential in changing the shape and balance of the breed, which, up until the early years of the 20th century, had been long in the back and low on the leg. The influential black bitch Jetson Bowdler won at Crufts in 1905, and her great-great-grandson Rocklyn Magic was widely used after the First World War as a sire of blacks. The blue roan dog Dixon Bowdler was the great-great-grandson of Fairholme Rally, root of all modern particolour Cockers. The blue roan dog Braeside Bustle was one of the earliest blue roans to achieve top winning status in what had been, until this time, the domain of the blacks. The breed shape had changed to a more balanced, shorter backed, higher on the leg type.

After the First World War, the breed became increasingly popular, frequently receiving the biggest breed entries at Crufts. Many of the famous Cocker kennels became established and made competition very stiff indeed. Mr H S Lloyd's of Ware Kennel was the dominant influence on the breed, and the Falconers Kennel of Mrs Jamieson Higgins and the Fulmer Kennel of Mrs Fytche also produced many top winners. In the 1930s, the breed prospered through the competition of many clever breeders. Mr Lloyd's dark blue roan dog, Lucky Star of Ware, twice won Best in Show at Crufts. The of Ware Kennel achieved further Best in Show wins at Crufts with Exquisite Model of Ware and Tracey Witch of Ware.

The Treetops, Sixshot, Misbourne, Lochranza and Broomleaf Kennels dominated the solid colours, while the Colinwood, of Ide, Weirdene and Merryworth Kennels added to the particoloured competition. The golden age of the Cocker Spaniel – from the 1940s to the 1950s – produced many beautiful specimens. The kennel names mentioned became pillars of the breed, and, if you traced back into any Cocker pedigree, you would be sure to find some of these bloodlines.

This brief history of the breed's development is very simplified, but credit must be given to the early breeders, who worked hard to achieve what we have today – the merry, sporting dog, a distinct variety of the Spaniel family – the Cocker. Among the Spaniel family, the Cocker is noted for its adaptability to town or country life and remains one of the most popular breeds in the UK. The Cocker is noted for his happy temperament and faithfulness to his owners.

THE AMERICAN COCKER SPANIEL

From the same root source, the American Cocker Spaniel has been bred. Slightly smaller than his British cousin, he has a more domed head and a shorter muzzle, a sloping topline and higher tail carriage. But the most noticeable difference is the abundance of coat which the American Cocker carries, making him both very glamorous and very demanding in terms of grooming requirements.

OTHER SPANIEL BREEDS

Another popular member of the Spaniel family, the English Springer Spaniel, is the tallest of the Spaniels, standing about 20 ins high at the shoulder. Popular as a working gundog, the English Springer is a very active dog, demanding plenty of exercise, but with the same soft, affectionate nature. Its most popular colour is liver and white, but black and white and tricolours are also popular.

Slightly smaller and with a finer

The English Springer: The tallest of the Spaniel breeds.

head than his English cousin, the Welsh Springer Spaniel is distinguished by his rich red and white coat. The breed is not quite as outgoing as the English Springer.

The Clumber Spaniel, long and low and principally white with lemon or orange markings, is the heaviest of the Spaniels, and has proven to be a successful gun dog and companion.

The Field Spaniel, once close to extinction, has enjoyed a resurgence in popularity in the show ring in recent years. Between the Cocker and the Springer in height, the Field's body is slightly longer for balance, and he has plenty of bone and substance. His head is beautiful, with skull, eyes and finely chiselled foreface which gives him great quality. Liver and black are the most popular

Above: The Welsh Springer: Distinguished by his rich, red colour.

Below: A Field Spaniel, with an eight-week-old Cocker Spaniel pup. The Field Spaniel is between the Cocker and the Springer in height.

colours, but roans, black and tans and liver and tans are occasionally seen. The Field has a loving, biddable temperament, but he is very happy as a working gundog and enjoys plenty of exercise.

The Sussex Spaniel is known for his substance, colour and rolling movement. At around 16 ins he is long, with a broad skull and a special frown to his expression. His beautiful colour – a gold-tipped coat of beautiful texture –

and his 'lowness to ground' identify him. Also a good worker, particularly useful for working in tough scrub and thick cover, like all Spaniels the Sussex needs plenty of freedom and exercise.

The Cocker's size and adaptability, his attractive head and expression, and his happy temperament have made him the most frequently seen Spaniel on the street.

The Cocker: The most popular of the Spaniel breeds.

2 *Choosing A Puppy*

Before going to choose a Cocker puppy, or, indeed, a puppy of any breed, you must consider that being a dog owner brings responsibilities and expense. A dog taken into the family is another mouth to feed and another demand on your time. You must be sure that you can fulfil these needs, that you can afford to feed the dog, to pay veterinary fees for inoculations and medical treatment, and to pay for boarding kennel accommodation during your holidays. Then there might be regular visits to the grooming parlour, and the time needed for taking your dog for walks and for grooming him. These are just a few of the demands that dog ownership brings. Having decided

Think carefully before taking on the responsibility of owning a dog.

that you are able and prepared to meet these needs, are you quite sure that the Cocker is the breed for you?

COCKER CHARACTERISTICS

The Cocker's height, about 16 ins, makes it adaptable to most households. The Cocker temperament – the merry, tail-wagging dog with adoring eyes on its owner and its eagerness to please – is perhaps what attracts most of the Cocker's following. But the Cocker is a sporting dog, and it demands and needs regular exercise. Whether you are a town dweller or a country dweller, you must be prepared to give your Cocker regular walks. The Cocker also grows coat, so the breed needs regular grooming for health and hygiene, and occasional trimming. You should be prepared to learn to trim your own dog, or to take him to a professional groom. If you are not daunted by any of these features, then you can be sure that a Cocker will reward your care with unfailing love and bring much pleasure into your life.

MALE OR FEMALE?

Perhaps the first consideration in choosing a puppy will be the preference for a dog or a bitch.

Years ago, it was often felt that bitches were more inconvenient because of their seasons, which meant twice-yearly periods of limited exercise and greater vigilance to guard off local canine suitors. Nowadays, seasons are less of a problem – injections are available which prevent the bitch from coming into season, or there is the option of neutering (spaying). Some people prefer bitches, feeling that they are more biddable and easier to house train. However, the decision on whether to choose a dog or a bitch is one of personal preference, for both have the same Cocker temperament and intelligence.

COLOUR

One of the many attractions of the Cocker Spaniel is the variety of attractive colours available. These can be divided into two broad sub-divisions: the solid colours and the particolours.

SOLIDS

BLACK: A favourite in the early days of the breed, and still very popular and successful in the show ring. Blacks often carry heavier coats than the particolours, and require more grooming.

RED AND GOLDEN: Perhaps the most popular colour, and it is a great joy to see the glistening golden coat and blond ears. The red is a deeper shade of gold. In recent years, there has been some adverse publicity regarding the temperament in some Cockers of this colour.

PARTICOLOURS

Particolours are a clearly marked black and white or orange with white; black, white and tan tricolours (something of a rarity); or the more intermingled colours of the roans – blue, orange and chocolate roan. The particolours often carry less feathering and coat than the solid colours.

Above: Solid colours: Black and golden.

Below: Orange roan: Particolours often have less feathering than the solid colours.

ACQUIRING A PUPPY

It is advisable to buy from a reputable breeder, rather than from a pet shop or a commercial kennel, who supply numerous breeds bought in from multiple outlets. Reputable breeders are those who have typical healthy Cockers, of good pedigree and temperament, and who use quality dogs as sires for the litters they breed.

REPUTABLE BREEDERS

How do you trace a reputable breeder? You can contact your national Kennel Club which will be able to supply names and addresses. Alternatively, you could buy one of the canine journals, where breeders may advertise. Cocker Spaniel Clubs will also help you to contact breeders in your area. Another way to find breeders is to visit a local dog show and speak to the Cocker exhibitors; this will give you a good idea of the breed's temperament and characteristics, and will also help you to decide on the colour you prefer. This is the way many potential pet owners make contact with their puppy's breeder.

CHOOSING YOUR PUPPY

Whether you are choosing a puppy as a family pet or as a potential show specimen, your priority is the same; a healthy, sound puppy of happy, extrovert temperament, well reared and with strong bones, bright shining eyes, a glossy coat, strong white teeth and clear, odour-free ears.

Avoid the shy, nervous puppy who does not play with his littermates or run up to greet you. You might feel sympathy for the smallest or frailest pup, and be tempted to pick him, but weaklings often bring problems with them.

The best time to look at Cocker puppies is when they are between

Blue roan (left) and liver roan.

Above: The best time to view puppies is when they are six to eight weeks of age.

Below: You will see the puppies' mother, and, hopefully, you will see other adult dogs from similar bloodlines.

six and eight weeks of age. By this time, they are beginning to look like miniature Cockers; they are beginning to run about and to develop temperament and character, and the particolours are beginning to show their markings and colour.

BUYING TO SHOW
If you intend to show your Cocker Spaniel, you should buy a puppy from a breeder who is successful in the showing world and is breeding from top-quality stock. The adage "You can't get a silk purse from a sow's ear" holds good where livestock is concerned. You should inform the breeder of

Watch the puppies playing together – this will give you an idea of their individual personalities.

your intentions at the time you choose the puppy. He might be able to provide a puppy of show potential, but no sensible breeder will guarantee show quality and success – so many things can go wrong during a puppy's formative months, and potential can be lost.

Puppies can lose bone, grow too big or not grow enough, for example; the list is endless, and the potentially beautiful swan can become the less beautiful duck! If you want a guaranteed show specimen, then you would do better to buy a youngster of about

If you are looking for a show prospect, the breeder will help assess potential.

eight months to a year old, if you can persuade the breeder to part with one. Of course, you will pay an appropriately higher price!

PREPARATIONS

Most breeders will not part with a puppy before he is eight weeks old, fully weaned from his mother and sturdy and bold enough to leave his littermates. However, before you collect your puppy there are a few essential preparations you need to make to ensure that your home and garden are safe, and you are fully equipped for your puppy's homecoming.

SLEEPING

Decide where your puppy will sleep, and establish his quarters – a box, basket or a crate. Puppies, like babies, need plenty of sleep, so a quiet spot in a warm place is important. A cardboard box with a blanket or towel inside, a safe cuddly toy or some old, tightly-knotted tights or socks will give the puppy a sense of companionship when he is feeling the loss of his littermates. Do not invest in expensive baskets until the puppy has gone through his teething stage! A strong cardboard box is just as effective, and much less expensive. Line your sleeping

A dog crate is an invaluable item of equipment.

box with thick newspaper, which is very absorbent, and invaluable in these early stages. Spread some sheets around his sleeping area in case of accidents during the night. A thick towel makes very suitable bedding for your puppy, with the advantage of being washable. Washable fleecy blankets or vetbeds are readily available on the market for sleeping accommodation.

When your puppy has passed his teething and destructive stage, you may wish to invest in something more stylish and permanent than a cardboard box. Dog baskets come in many sizes and types, but choose one which will be comfortable for your fully-grown Cocker. There are some strong plastic 'indestructible' baskets on the market, which are washable and hygienic. There are also soft washable duvet baskets available, which seem very comfortable for the dog. Whichever you choose, it is important to change the bedding regularly and to wash the basket, to prevent odours and to keep your dog's bed free from flea or mite infestations.

A relatively recent development in canine accommodation which has spread from the show world to the domestic scene is the crate. Dog crates are becoming widely available in the UK, and are very useful. They are usually made of strong steel; they are collapsible, and have a sleeping tray in the base. The puppy or adult can be enclosed inside for sleeping, when non-doggy visitors call, or for feeding. They are also invaluable for helping with house training. Dogs will rarely soil their own beds unless neglected for too long, so, if the puppy is taken from his crate to the garden, he will soon get into the toilet habit.

When the puppy wakes from his sleep, take him outside to the designated toilet training area, let him relieve himself, and praise him when he does – you are well on the way to house training. Dogs acquire their routines quite quickly, and Cockers are intelligent, quick learners.

FEEDING BOWLS

A special type of bowl is available for Spaniels to prevent them dangling their long ears in their food and water. These high-sided, narrow-topped bowls are called Spaniel bowls, and are most useful. Again, hygiene is important so choose a stainless steel or a porcelain bowl. The heavier bowls are less likely to be tipped or knocked over by your boisterous and hungry pet!

COLLAR AND LEAD

Personally, I do not like to see very young puppies wearing collars and leads. For the first month or so after you acquire your puppy, he should be kept within your own territory until his course of inoculations is finished. You may wish to train him a little during this period, to accustom him to the feeling of a collar and the control of a lead. Ensure that the collar is comfortable, not too tight nor too slack; 'gentle' is the key word. Do not drag your puzzled puppy along: encourage him with kind words; make his early lead training a game and he will soon prove to be biddable and happy on his collar and lead.

TOYS

Mental stimulation for your puppy can be provided by games and toys. A tightly-knotted pair of tights or socks can provide much entertainment. A hard rubber ball, which is non-chewable and too big to be swallowed, will also be popular. Hide chews, especially knotted ones, are useful at teething time.

Do not allow your puppy to carry or retrieve stones; they can easily be swallowed or cause damage to his teeth.

COLLECTING YOUR PUPPY

At last, the big day arrives, and it is time to collect your puppy. It is easy to get carried away in all the excitement, so make a list of the things your want to check with the breeder.

You will need to check that the puppies have been wormed, and find out which worming preparation was used. You will need to continue the worming programme, and continuity of medication is preferred.

The breeder should provide you with a diet sheet to guide you through the rearing of your puppy. Many breeders will also provide you with enough food for the puppy's first few meals.

You should also bring away with you the pedigree certificate and Kennel Club registration for your puppy. Buying a puppy which is not Kennel Club registered, or which is from

Above: The big day arrives when it is time to collect your puppy.

Below: Give your puppy a chance to settle in his new home.

parents who are unregistered, brings complications if you later wish to register your puppy, show him or breed from him.

THE JOURNEY HOME

Taking your puppy away from his familiar surroundings, his mother and his littermates will be a traumatic experience for him, but with sensible handling, the transition to his new home can be made as stress-free as possible. Remember your puppy will probably not have been outside his home environment so everything will be strange to him – sights, sounds, smells, the vibration of the car engine. If you are driving, do not go alone to fetch your puppy, who should be held gently on the journey home until he becomes accustomed to the surroundings, when he will usually nod off to sleep!

ARRIVING HOME

Again, your home is new to the puppy, and he should be introduced to his territory. If he is to be restricted to certain rooms of your house, then introduce him to those rooms only. Do not rush it, and do not let over-enthusiastic children or visitors overawe the puppy with noise and too much handling, Teach children how to pick up and hold a puppy, gently and securely, and how to put the puppy down on the floor gently – never dropping him. A wriggling, energetic puppy can soon escape from a young child's grasp, so you should exercise great vigilance. Children are often unaware of their own strength and roughness when handling a puppy, and this can ruin your new puppy's temperament.

THE FIRST NIGHT

Introduce your puppy to his sleeping quarters well before bedtime. Let him have his meals and naps in this area, then he will become accustomed to it as his area. He is likely to cry for his mother and littermates on the first few nights. You may choose to go and comfort him, but it would be unwise to take him to your bedroom if you do not want to allow him there on a regular basis. Like children, dogs soon acquire habits and you should work at getting your puppy into the routines which are going to be his regular way of life.

3 Rearing Your Puppy

Having acquired your Cocker Spaniel puppy, you must now establish a sensible routine of good rearing and good habits, so that your Cocker will grow up healthy and well-balanced.

THE FIRST FEW WEEKS

Until now, your puppy has been living with his mother and littermates. At eight weeks of age, he is taken away to a new, strange and bewildering environment. It is important that you take care to socialise the puppy in this new environment. He may be nervous and frightened of strange objects and noises, and he may be unaccustomed to children. Be sensible. If you have children, do not let them maul and over-handle the puppy. Teach them how to pick him up and put him down correctly and gently.

FEEDING

The breeder of your puppy should have given you a diet sheet, and it would be wise to adhere to this for a while and avoid sudden changes of diet, which could upset the puppy's digestion, usually causing diarrhoea.

The complete, balanced diet – usually in a biscuit or meal form – is becoming increasingly used by breeders, because of its

Take time to socialise your puppy in his new environment.

If you feed a complete diet, make sure drinking water is always available.

convenience and its scientifically tested, balanced ingredients. I am rather old-fashioned, and believe that dogs enjoy meat, and some variety in their diet, and I tend to feed my dogs accordingly. It is a matter for the individual owner. However, what is important is that the young puppy is fed regularly, in small amounts, usually starting with four small meals a day at eight weeks of age. The frequency of his meals should be gradually reduced to one main meal a day by the time he is one year old.

If you choose the complete food option, you should follow the manufacturer's instructions carefully. If you want to vary the diet, the guiding principle is a mixture of carbohydrate and protein. The following diets might be followed:

EIGHT WEEKS TO FOUR MONTHS

Four meals per day.
Breakfast: Milky meal consisting of cereals and warm milk, rice pudding or scrambled egg.
Midday: Small amount of finely chopped meat – chicken or carefully boned fish, mixed with soaked puppy meal.
Late afternoon: Repeat breakfast-type meal.
Late night: As midday.

Finely chopped, cooked or raw vegetables are a useful addition. Always soak dog meal with boiling water or gravy and allow to cool. Since meal swells, this soaking avoids overfeeding and aids digestion. Occasional hard, dry biscuits can be given to aid teething. If you wish to give your dog a bone, which can help with teething and give him hours of pleasure, make sure it is a large beef or lamb bone. Poultry bones are fine, brittle, easily swallowed and can cause internal damage.

FOUR MONTHS TO EIGHT MONTHS

Divide the food into three equal amounts. By now, your puppy may be losing interest in milky foods, so a fish or meat meal may be given three times a day. This should consist of about 4 oz meat or fish per meal, and up to two handfuls of meal. Leftover meat and vegetables can be used; these add variety, but you should reduce the usual food amounts accordingly

EIGHT MONTHS ONWARDS

Feed your Cocker twice daily, with, perhaps, the occasional drink of milk or cereals and milk if he seems to require it. Cockers grow rapidly, and your puppy's body weight and general condition will tell you whether you are giving him enough – he should be well covered, but not fat or skinny! A daily vitamin and mineral supplement is useful during these growing days, and I have always fed my dogs with a couple of brewer's yeast tablets daily. They are a good source of vitamin B, and, besides, the dogs enjoy them!

By the time your Cocker Spaniel is 12 months of age, he should have just one meal a day.

GROOMING

The Cocker Spaniel is a long-coated breed, and so regular grooming is essential. It is important that your puppy gets used to this at an early stage, and then he will learn to enjoy the attention, which will make the task easier. Teach him to stand on a non-slip table, while you gently brush and comb through all of his head, ears and body. Praise him when you have finished. For more information on grooming, see Chapter Four.

WORMING

All puppies need to be treated for roundworm, and, in most cases, this is a matter of continuing the worming programme started by the puppy's breeder. Generally puppies are wormed at six weeks and eight weeks of age. You may wish to worm him at about four months old, and you should consult your vet when you take him for his important inoculations.

INOCULATIONS

You should take your puppy to be inoculated against the canine

Your vet will advise on a programme of inoculations.

diseases hepatitis, leptospirosis and parvovirus. Any of these could prove fatal to a dog, so it is essential to protect your pet. Most vets will not inoculate until the puppy is ten weeks of age. Usually, two visits to the vet are necessary, at about two weeks apart, and you should not allow your puppy out of the confines of your home and garden, or to have contact with other dogs, until after the inoculations are complete.

SOCIALISATION

It is important to handle the

puppy gently, to build up his confidence and to forge the bond between dog and owner in the early days. Gentle stroking, talking to the puppy and gentle grooming are important elements of socialisation. Allow the puppy to experience the everyday noises of household routine – the television, vacuum cleaner, washing machine, and so on – but do it gradually, and take care that you do not frighten the puppy by taking him by surprise more than is avoidable. Take your puppy for his first car ride; perhaps on your knee for the first try, but on later trips, the puppy should be placed where you intend him to travel for the rest of his life.

After his inoculation you should take him out to see life – to the park, the local shops, to meet strangers, see traffic and to meet other dogs. You should take care that these meetings are carefully supervised – ensure that the other dogs are as sociable and as friendly as your Cocker. A wide variety of experiences, carefully managed, should help make your Cocker a confident and happy pet.

EXERCISE

Cockers are sporting dogs and they love their exercise. From four months of age, your Cocker can be lead-trained and taken for short walks, but take care not to over-exercise him while he is still

Spaniels are natural retrievers, and this game is an endless source of fun.

Spaniels love swimming and this is also a great form of exercise.

growing. He will enjoy running free, but make sure he is in a safe environment and will return to you on command before you let him off the lead for exercise. In wet weather, your dog still needs his walks, and you should keep a towel for his use on return. Towel him dry, or use a chamois leather wrung out in hot water, to absorb all the dampness. If you have invested in a crate, he can dry off by resting in his crate on dry towels in a warm, draught-free place. This saves the wet kitchen floor, the paw marks on the carpet and the damp doggy smell!

A puppy's attention span is limited, so keep training sessions short.

TRAINING YOUR COCKER

Your Cocker Spaniel is a new member of your family and, in order for him to fit in well with your family and in society, he must be trained to know what is acceptable and unacceptable in his behaviour.

The Cocker is a very biddable dog, only too eager to please and quick to learn. Cockers have competed successfully in Obedience tests and in Agility trials, and, if you wish to pursue these specialist areas, then you can join a local club, which will help you with advanced training in these areas. However, all dogs need a moderate level of obedience to make them easy to live with – house training, initially, then lead training and the rudiments of obedience – and these can all be taught by the average owner.

TRAINING GUIDELINES

All the basic training exercises are possible for the novice owner. It is largely a matter of patience and common sense.

Make the training sessions short, as puppies have only short concentration spans. Do not bore the puppy with overlong sessions.

Make the sessions fun and

reward your puppy after a good session. Use bait or tidbits to keep him concentrating and interested.

End your session at a good point, when you have been successful and he has been praised.

HOUSE TRAINING

The first task is to make your Cocker clean in the house, to teach him that fouling indoors is not allowed. This is usually a simple task, quickly learned by the young Cocker.

Always take your puppy outside after all meals. Decide on what is an acceptable toilet area in your garden, and watch him until he does the business! Praise him when he does. Repeat this performance after every meal and first thing in the morning.

To avoid overnight accidents in the early days, I recommend that your puppy is crated at bedtime in one of the collapsible crates mentioned earlier. Very few dogs will foul their own sleeping area, and this is one way of avoiding overnight accidents, but remember, let the puppy out last thing at night and first thing in the morning.

If your puppy is sleeping in a box or a basket, then you can place thick sheets of newspaper near the door so that any accident can be contained in that area. This 'paper training' can be extended into the garden so that the puppy learns where he is allowed to relieve himself.

If you see your puppy having an accident, scold him with a firm "No" and put him outside, into the acceptable area. Careful training can only be effective at the time of the crime, so do not scold your puppy on the discovery of an accident long after it has happened, because he will not know what he is being scolded for.

BOUNDARY TRAINING

By this, I mean teaching the puppy to know where he is allowed and what he is allowed to do. Is he allowed upstairs? Is he allowed to sit on furniture? Is he allowed to jump at yourself or visitors? It is never too early to start training, and this can be done with the power of your voice. Firm commands of "No!" and corrective action will bring quick results, so, if the puppy is climbing on to a sofa and he is not allowed to, you should give the command "No!", and firmly place the puppy back on to the floor. The same applies if your puppy jumps up, which is a natural trait

Good manners are essential so work hard at training your pet to behave well in all situations.

with the affectionate Cocker, who will greet his owner and all visitors enthusiastically. Remember that some of your friends might not be as dog-friendly as you are, and might not welcome the serrated tights, the dog hairs and the paw prints on clothes. Give the negative command, and the gentle but firm push to the floor, and he will soon know what is expected.

SIT

Perhaps the most useful command to control a dog, and one which is easy to teach. With the command word "Sit", apply gentle pressure

Build up the Stay exercise in easy stages.

on top of the hindquarters, in front of the tail, and put the dog in a sitting position. Praise him when he has successfully completed the exercise, and repeat a few times.

STAY

This is a natural progression from the Sit command. Use the command "Stay" as you move a couple of paces from the dog, always facing him and pointing at the "Stay" position as you say the word. Then teach him to Come by calling his name, or using the command "Come". Praise him and repeat the exercise, gradually increasing the distance between yourself and the dog.

LEADS

There are many types of lead available. The traditional collar and lead gives fair control; the choke chain is stronger and more severe, but a good corrective aid against dogs who pull on the lead. The show lead, made of nylon or leather, is light but is not recommended for strong control, especially in boisterous, untrained puppies.

In more recent years, the harness has been favoured by some, as giving more central control with the lead attachment fixed to a body harness. I feel that this is very restrictive for the dog, and quite unnecessary. I am often perturbed to see the tightness of some of these, restricting the dog's breathing.

Head collars with leads attached have also been marketed, and I dislike these too, for their potential to be very severe with the dog's head, and so to restrict the dog's breathing and panting. And, if the unfortunate wearer were attacked by another dog, he could do little to defend himself.

For young puppies, I favour a light nylon collar and lead, or a nylon show lead for training in the garden. For adult dogs, I use a nylon rope-type choke lead, which is soft and strong.

LEAD TRAINING

An unruly dog, pulling his owner about on the end of a lead, twisting from side to side, is a real nuisance and no pleasure to take for a walk. Lead training can start at about three or four months of age. Before this time, puppies are usually confined to their home territory until after inoculations. Apart from lead training, puppies should not be given much exercise before they are six months of age.

Before the inoculation course has been completed, you can accustom your puppy to a collar and lead within the confines of the garden.

Your Cocker Spaniel should learn to walk on a lead without pulling. If you aim to compete in Obedience, you will need to achieve a higher standard of control.

Like babies, puppies need a lot of sleep and good food during these early growing months. Too much exercise can cause spindly bone and weedy bodies.

First lead training sessions can be hilarious, with the puppy doing all he can to escape or cause havoc. Give him plenty of slack lead, and gradually bring him under control with the command "Heel" or "Walk".

For dogs who pull persistently, you could use a choke chain to pull him back to heel, but use a gentle type of lead with large links. Be sure to put on the chain correctly, with the lead ring on the right hand side of the neck, so that, with your dog on your left side, the ring pulls upwards when tightened and releases immediately when slackened. When the puppy pulls, jerk him back with the positive command "Heel!". Once you have mastered controlled walking, you can start using a gentler lead. Choke chains are rarely needed permanently on a Cocker.

ADVANCED TRAINING

The Cocker is an intelligent and biddable dog who learns quickly and is eager to please. For owners who wish to enjoy these traits of their dog's temperament, there is the opportunity to engage in Obedience classes and competitions and Agility training.

Obedience training classes are a very popular pastime and you can usually find details of those in your area from your veterinary surgery, local newspaper or police station. If you have problems, contact the Kennel Club, who will advise you of your nearest classes.

Agility work, which involves the dog and his owner tackling a course of obstacles such as jumps, weaving poles and tunnels, can be great fun but demand a fit and athletic dog and an energetic owner. This activity has become increasingly popular during the last few years and is now often staged at many dog shows. Again, you can find our about your local centres from the same sources as for the obedience classes.

Cockers take readily to both Obedience and Agility work and I have been delighted to see a Cocker of my own breeding, an orange and white dog sold as a family pet, do very well in these competitions.

4 Grooming And Trimming

As a long-coated breed, Cocker Spaniels need regular grooming and trimming to keep them healthy, hygienic and looking at their best. Regular brushing and combing is required to keep the coat tangle-free and unmatted. The skin is stimulated by grooming, and your dog's coat should look shiny and glossy if he is in good condition. A dull coat without bloom usually suggests worms or a dietary shortcoming, and you should visit the vet if this is the case.

EQUIPMENT

You will need the following equipment:

- A soft brush (for head and body).
- A No. 6 comb (to remove body undercoat and loose back hair).
- A metal pin brush (for ears and leg feathering).
- A small pair of scissors (for removing hair from inside the ears and from underneath the foot).
- A hand glove or piece of velvet (for finishing off and to give a glossy shine).

EARLY GROOMING

Start gently but firmly, by brushing from head to tail with the soft brush. Then, gently brush through the ears and leg feathering with the metal pin brush. If there are any cotters, tease them out with your fingers. Do not pull too much on the brush; this will hurt the puppy and make him dislike his grooming sessions. Keep his eyes clean by wiping with a damp tissue or cotton wool. Keep ears clear of wax with a cotton bud.

Puppies carry little feathering in the first months, so grooming need only take a couple of minutes. Train your puppy to

Accustom your puppy to grooming from an early age.

grooming equipment. Discourage this behaviour with a firm "No" and a tap to the nose. It is vital to let him know who is in control. A puppy going unchecked at this stage can develop into a real nuisance.

I was once horrified to receive a phone call from some clients, telling me that their Cocker was vicious, biting them when they attempted to groom him. I visited the house and found that this was true. The puppy's behaviour had been unchecked in the early weeks, followed by less than regular attempts to groom him, and then heightened aggression when they did try. The dog had taken control, and his owners were frightened of him. A firm hand is necessary early on in such cases. Be firm should there be any sign of such behaviour.

stand or sit, as required. Later, you can train him to lie on his side while you brush his tummy and nether parts.

During these early grooming sessions, it is important to establish control over the puppy. Some puppies take a dislike to brush or comb, often through uncertainty, and might attempt to bite your fingers or gnaw at the

THE ADULT COCKER

The mature Cocker will carry a fair amount of feathering on his ears, legs and body, and, if he is well trained from an early age, grooming is an easy matter. However, if you neglect regular grooming, you will have to cope with a matted, cottered coat, and you will have made life more difficult and less pleasant for both

The mature Cocker Spaniel has considerable feathering and this must be groomed regularly to prevents mats and tangles from forming.

yourself and the dog. In the same way, you can hardly take your dog to a grooming parlour in a neglected state, and expect them to remedy weeks of neglect with a single trim. Grooming should be a regular, ongoing event.

BATHING
When I owned my first Cocker, the general advice was to bath dogs very rarely, say once every six months. Attitudes have changed, and, with a host of good shampoos on the market, dogs will not lose coat condition from regular bathing. My house-dogs are bathed every week, their ears and teeth are checked, their nails clipped (if needed), and they are blow-dried with a hairdryer. The whole routine takes about one hour, and is little effort for keeping your dogs in a clean, healthy condition.

Before bathing your dog, groom him thoroughly to see that his coat is free from knots and tangles. Decide where you will bath him. Do you use your own bathroom, or a large sink in the utility room, if one is available? You may choose to bath your dog in his own portable bath in the garage.

Take care to ensure that the water is not too hot. Handle your Cocker gently and calmly, especially during his first experiences of being bathed. So often, one hears people saying that their dog hates being bathed, but this is often the result of unpleasant early experiences. There is no need to use too much water in the bath; a jug can be used to soak your dog's coat.

Before starting the soaking process, place small wads of cotton wool in the dog's ears to prevent water entering the ear canals. Remove these when drying the dog. Soak the dog, taking care not to allow soapy water into his eyes, then apply the shampoo, working from head to tail. There is no need to spend a fortune on some of the hugely-priced specialist dog shampoos. A good-quality shampoo for humans will suffice, or there are some good medicated insecticidal shampoos available from pet stores and superstores. Follow the instructions and shampoo the dog gently and thoroughly. Talk to him to reassure him.

Drain the water from the bath and rinse the dog in clean warm water, and then squeeze the excess water from his coat. Lift him from the bath and wrap him in a clean, dry towel, and rub him firmly until he is damp-dry. Then use a hairdryer to dry him thoroughly. The noise and draught from the hairdryer may upset the dog initially, but if you reassure him he

will soon grow accustomed to it and enjoy the warmth. Do not hold the hairdryer too close, so that the dog does not get burned or become uncomfortably hot. Brush or comb your dog while drying. Comb out the section of the coat you are drying and you will find that it dries straight and glossy.

Make sure that your Cocker is thoroughly dry before bedding him down for the night. Sleeping in damp conditions is not beneficial or comfortable for the dog, and can cause colds and other ailments.

ROUTINE CARE

EARS
In the past, Spaniels had a reputation for being prone to ear problems. To some extent, this is a myth. Any ear can be prone to problems if it does not receive regular attention. Ears should be clean, pinkish in colour and odour-free. You can keep the airway free from excess hair by clipping carefully round the inside of the ear opening. Then, clean the ear with moist cotton wool or a baby bud. Do not probe deeply into the ear, as this can cause internal damage. Cleansing ear

drops are available from your vet or from good pet shops.

EYES

Keep your pet's eyes clear of crusty discharge or pus by wiping daily with damp cotton wool. I have been told that wiping with a used teabag is beneficial and helps to prevent tear staining, but I have no scientific evidence for this. Nevertheless, I use this method! It is certainly soft on the eye, if nothing else.

NAILS

Young puppies need their nails trimming regularly as they grow; they are needle-sharp and quite fine, and easy to trim with human nail-clippers. As the dog grows older the nails thicken, and regular exercise on hard surfaces should obviate the need for trimming nails, but, if this is necessary, you can acquire some nail-clippers from a good pet shop.

Avoid cutting off too much and causing the nail to bleed. In light-coloured nails, you can see the quick, and you should not cut back this far. The safest way of keeping your dog's nails in trim is to cut back little and often.

TEETH

Keep your Cocker's mouth healthy and his breath odour-free by

If needed, trim the nails with nail clippers.

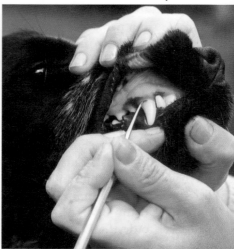

If plaque accumulates, it will have to be removed with a tooth-scaler.

regular attention to the teeth. You can brush your dog's teeth with an ordinary toothbrush and toothpaste (canine toothpaste is also available at pet shops and through your vet). In this way you can avoid the build-up of yellow tartar on the teeth, keep the gums healthy and avoid food being lodged in the folds of the lips, which gives rise to a very unpleasant odour which will require veterinary treatment.

TRIMMING

Canine hairdressing is not only to keep the dog looking good, but to keep his coat, skin, tail, ears and mouth in a healthy state.

For many people, trimming is the domain of the specialist, and they prefer to take their Cocker to a trimming parlour at regular intervals. Some people take their Cocker back to the breeder, who might be prepared to trim puppies he has bred, or who will recommend a trimmer who specialises in Spaniels. If you decide to use a trimming parlour, ensure that the proprietors know how Cocker Spaniels should be trimmed, and make it clear how you want your dog trimmed. The Cocker Spaniel's coat is maintained most easily and looks

Some pet dogs may be clipped, which is quick and efficient, but the effect can be a little severe.

its best when it is hand-trimmed, rather like plucking a turkey. This gives a flat, glossy coat. However, this is a specialist art, and very time-consuming. It is certainly the method required for a show Spaniel. Many grooming parlours use electric clippers and thinning scissors, which are quicker and give a more severe trim. Once a coat has been clipped it is hard to get back the natural flatness and gloss; the coat often going woolly after such treatment. However, it is the method preferred by some owners who do not like grooming, or who want the minimum of hair on the dog, especially in bad weather, when

1. Before stripping: The aim of hand stripping is to thin the coat layers in order to achieve a clean outline.

2. Comb or rake the coat to remove any loose hair.

4. Thinning scissors can be used on the ears to reduce the bulk, making sure there is no evidence of scissor marks.

3. Starting with the skull, the finger and thumb method is used to 'pull' the coat.

5. Continue hand-stripping along the back and topline.

6. Move on to the side of the neck, the shoulders and the body.

8. Use thinning scissors to trim the chest.

7. Lightly 'pull' the hair over the upper thigh, blending it with the shorter body coat, and the longer feathering of the underline.

9. Trim the hair on the tail to give a neat appearance.

10. The upper thighs may need thinning.

12. Hair growing between the pads must be removed.

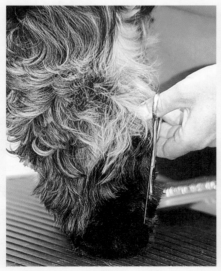

11. Trim the hair on the hocks, but not to excess.

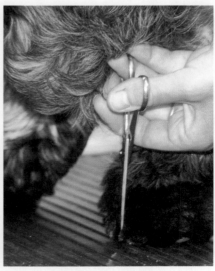

13. Trim around the feet to give a round, compact appearance.

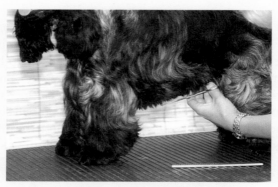

14. The underline can be lightly finished.

15. The end result – ready for the show ring.

wet paws and feathering bring mud and dirt into the house.

Thinning scissors are less severe than the electric clipper, but, again, once trimmed in this manner, it is often necessary to carry on in the same way to keep the coat in trim.

HAND-TRIMMING

Hand-trimming is an ongoing practice and not something which can be tackled in one trimming session. Most Cocker exhibitors use this method, and keep their dogs in trim with a weekly session. Once perfected, it is quite straightforward as long as the coat is ready for pulling and you have strong fingers. The most important thing to remember is to pull with the direction of the coat, and you must not attempt pulling when the coat is not ready.

The Cocker puppy might carry a heavy, woolly-textured profusion of puppy coat on his legs and back. As this changes to adult coat, the puppy coat becomes slacker and can be plucked out by gripping between thumb and forefinger. Start on the back of the neck and gradually work along the back to the root of the tail. It takes time and practice, but it will come! Do not do it all in one

session, but, in puppyhood, perhaps for twenty minutes at a time. It is unlikely to be ready for pulling before your puppy is eight months of age. Once the puppy coat is out, you will see a flat, glossy coat underneath and subsequent trimmings will be much easier.

STEP-BY-STEP GUIDE
EARS

You can hand-trim the outside of the tops of the ears to help the ear lie close to the head and to hang well, or you might use thinning scissors to trim out this thick hair. If you use thinning scissors, choose a pair with one plain blade and one serrated blade, and trim underneath the top hair, not on the surface. Keep the serrated blade uppermost and do a little at a time, combing out the loose hair after every cutting.

FRONT

Using thinning scissors in this way, you can trim the breast and chest of the dog, extending to the chest bone.

UNDER THE TAIL

For hygiene and neatness, you can trim under the tail in the same manner.

HOCKS

The back lower part of the rear legs (the hocks) tend to grow thick hair, and again this can be thinned out, but not excessively, as this can make the dog look spindly. Trim up the hocks and under the top coat, but leave the hocks well covered.

FEET

The Cocker's feet should be round, tight and compact, and this can be enhanced by good trimming. With sharp, straight-edged scissors, trim under the foot and remove all hair that protrudes between the pads. Then, trim the top and sides of the foot, trimming across the toes, not up them.

PRACTICE

Do not expect to be a great trimmer at your first attempt. It takes time, practice and patience. Early attempts could look awful, but fear not, hair grows again! These basic guidelines for trimming might help to keep your dog tidy, but, if you want to keep your dog in show ring standard trim, and would like to do it yourself, then it would be advisable to ask a local exhibitor if you could watch him or her trimming and learn some techniques. Alternatively, you might prefer to have your dog professionally trimmed. Whichever you choose, regular grooming will help all concerned.

5 Showing Your Cocker

ost Cocker owners never have any intention of showing, and many drift into it by chance – so, some words of advice. Before becoming seriously involved in the world of dog showing, it is essential that your Cocker is a specimen of show quality. If he is not, the pursuit will be one of endless disappointment, such is the competition in the Cocker rings at dog shows. Many people are tempted to show their Cocker, having had him admired in the street or perhaps at a local pet show.

From there, they might go on to try the bigger shows run under Kennel Club rules. Some people become absorbed by the competition world, some might try it and opt out, and, for others, it becomes a way of life: a weekly routine of trimming, bathing and travelling to shows in pursuit of prize cards and rosettes.

TYPES OF SHOW
There are several categories of shows in the UK.

Exemption Shows: So called because they are exempt from many of the rules of the Kennel Club, the governing body of the

Showing is an absorbing hobby, but you must be confident that you have a dog of suitable quality.

canine world. These shows usually consist of a few classes for pedigree dogs and some for pedigree and crossbreeds. They are informal, and, for many, are the starting point in the showing game. These shows are often run in conjunction with local charity fairs or small agricultural shows. Entries are made on the day of the show.

Sanction And Limited shows: These are organised by local dog clubs and are open to members. You are able to join when you enter your dog in the show. Dogs who have won a Challenge Certificate (the award which counts towards making a dog into a Champion) are not allowed to compete. These shows usually consist of 20 to 60 classes.

Open Shows: These are usually bigger and attract more entries. There are likely to be breed classes for Cocker Spaniels. Champions and Challenge Certificate winners are allowed to compete.

General Championship Shows: The biggest type of show, and Challenge Certificates are on offer. Known as CCs, these awards are the most coveted and are won by the best male and female in each breed. Once a dog has been awarded three such awards, won

under different judges, he is eligible for the title of Champion, or, in the case of the gundog breeds, the title of Show Champion, often marked as Sh. Ch. on pedigrees. For a Cocker Spaniel, or any other gun dog breed, the dog must win an award of merit at a Field Trial to show that he has working ability before he can become a full Champion.

Breed Club Shows: Organised by breed clubs, these offer classes for one specific breed, for example, the Cocker Spaniel. A visit to one of these shows is often a good way of seeing the quality of the breed, and of ascertaining whether your own dog is of show quality.

Different countries have different categories of shows, the most prestigious being the Championship shows, where the awards necessary to make a Champion are competed for. Your national Kennel Club will provide definitions and rules for the types of show available to you. The canine press, in any country, is the place to find publicity for forthcoming shows.

ENTERING YOUR DOG

Before you can enter your dog in any type of show, except the

Exemption Show, you must have him registered at the Kennel Club, which is usually done by the puppy's breeder and transferred to your name.

You will find notification of all dog shows in the weekly canine press. You must write to the club secretary and ask for a schedule to enter your dog in the appropriate class or classes, which are defined in the schedule.

1. Hold the head in place, lift by the chest and place the fore feet down, slightly apart.

IS YOUR DOG GOOD ENOUGH?

Go to a show, look at the dogs on exhibition, talk to the exhibitors. If your dog has come from a breeder who is also a regular exhibitor, ask for his or her opinion. If you decide to have a go at showing, you must consider trimming and presenting the dog to look his best, which is described later, and then both you and your dog must acquire a little ring training and etiquette.

2. If needed, correct and straighten each foreleg.

RING TRAINING CLASSES

These classes are found in all areas, and your local vet will often know the details. If not, phone a local breeder. Most breeders and exhibitors use these classes, often held in the evening, to introduce their young stock and hopefuls to the etiquette of the show ring. By

3. Still keeping the head in place, move your hand down the body to the rear end and position the hindlegs.

4. *Adjust the lead to the correct position.*

5. *The correct show pose.*

6. *Some experienced exhibitors prefer to pose their dog without the lead.*

attending these, your dog will become accustomed to other dogs, and will learn how to stand in the show position and how to move for the judge's assessment. He will also become accustomed to being handled by judges and others – all essential, if your dog is to have any chance of success.

WHAT THE JUDGE LOOKS FOR
All breeds are judged according to their Breed Standard. The Breed Standard is the template of the breed, produced by serious breeders in the early days of the breed, and detailing the physical features which make a Cocker Spaniel a typical specimen of that breed. The judge is looking for a dog who conforms to these essentials. The judge will handle your dog to assess his conformation – his bone structure and anatomy. The skeletal engineering of the dog is essential as this is what gives him a healthy body and sound movement.

Whole books have been written on this subject, and, if you become seriously involved in exhibiting, breeding and judging, it would benefit you to invest in some of these.

As you will see, judges are not just looking for superficial beauty

points, but sound functional anatomy. Serious breeders regard this as highly important when choosing their breeding stock and picking their own future show prospects.

ESSENTIALS OF THE BREED

GENERAL APPEARANCE
The Cocker Spaniel is sturdy, well-boned and solidly built, and his body is essentially square.

TEMPERAMENT
Cocker temperament is what has made it such a popular breed. The merry Cocker, with ever-wagging tail, eager to please and loving life, is the nature of the breed. There is no fun in living with a nervous dog, and aggressive Cockers should never be tolerated; these traits are quite alien to Cocker temperament.

HEAD AND SKULL
The head of the Cocker is oblong in shape, divided into two balanced parts: the skull, which is slightly domed, not too broad, and clean-cheeked; and the muzzle, which is oblong, quite deep and with soft flews which are not too heavy. These two oblongs are divided by a 'stop', an

indentation between the eyes which puts the two oblongs of the head on parallel planes.

EYES

The Standard is quite detailed on this point. They should be full, and dark in colour. With the liver colours, a dark hazel colour is required to harmonise with coat colour. The liver and tan roan, which is a comparatively rare colour, is genetically linked to a lighter shade of eye. The expression of intelligence and gentleness is often soulful, endearing and expresses the faithful nature of the breed.

EARS

A distinguishing feature of the Spaniel breeds, the Cocker's ear leather should run to the end of the muzzle. Feathering on the ear often lengthens the appearance considerably. More important, perhaps, is the set of the ear, adjoining the head at the level of the eye. A high-set ear alters the expression and detracts from the quality of the head and is often found with a broad, flat skull.

The typical expression of gentleness and intelligence.

The ears, a feature of the breed, should run to the end of the muzzle.

*The teeth should meet in
a perfect scissor bite.*

MOUTH

While minor teeth faults do not
affect the appearance of the dog or
detract from his value as a family
pet, a Cocker with a mouth fault
should not be considered as a
show specimen.

NECK

'Moderate' is the key word where
the neck is concerned. The Cocker
Spaniel is an unexaggerated breed.
Overlong necks might be eye-
catching, but often unbalance the
Cocker. Short necks are often the
result of poor shoulders. The neck
should be long enough to give a
balanced outline, and strong
enough to enable the dog to pick
up and carry a bird.

FOREQUARTERS

The shoulder blade and upper arm
form a lever system, which

determines the length of neck of
the dog, the width of chest and
the length of the dog's stride. The
ideal is a shoulder blade set at an
angle of 45 degrees to the
horizontal, and an upper arm of
almost equal length to the
shoulder blade, set at a right angle
to the shoulder blade. An upright
shoulder often brings a short
upright upper arm, a narrow chest
and a short neck. Good shoulder
angulation usually brings a length
of stride when the dog moves
which is economical and desirable
in a sporting dog.

BODY

Short-backed, square, big-ribbed,
with a rounded rump and low-set
tail – these are the essential
features of the Cocker's body. The
depth of body should be about
equal to the length of leg, to give
a balanced appearance. The body
length is taken up largely by the
rib cage. This is made up of
thirteen pairs of ribs, forming the
substructure of the body. It is
important that the ribs are well-
sprung and deep, reaching to the
level of the elbow, to give the dog
good lung and heart room. The
rib cage should take up most of
the dog's body space, and the area
between the last rib and the

hindquarters should be short. This area is called the 'couplings', and a Cocker should be short-coupled. The couplings are an important area in working with the lever system of the hindquarters – part of the muscular power which drives the dog along.

HINDQUARTERS
The hindquarters provide the motoring power of the Cocker. A well-turned stifle and broad thighs are desirable. The rump is gently rounded with the tail set just below the level of the back.

The judge will be looking for a well curved back leg with good turn of stifle. This is created by the length and angulation of the underlying bones. The upper thighbone, the femur, should be long and laid back at about 45 degrees, with the bones of the lower thigh (tibia and fibula) of almost equal length and forming a 90 degree angle with the upper thigh. This construction will bring a low hock joint, which is an important driving mechanism in the dog's movement. Upright bones will alter the shape of the dog's rear leg, making it straight (called a straight stifle) with narrow thighs and high hocks, which are not only less pleasing to

the eye, but represent an ineffective mechanism for movement.

FEET
Thick, round, well-padded, cat-like feet are essential for a dog bred originally as a gundog to work over all sorts of rough terrain. Thin, open feet are more prone to injury and lameness. While exercise might improve feet and pasterns, and clever trimming can disguise bad feet, good feet should be bred for and are an inherited trait.

TAIL
It is the choice of the breeder whether the Cocker is docked or not. Cockers who are not docked are seen more frequently now, but rarely in show rings in the UK. The long tail tends to unbalance the appearance of the short, compact Cocker, and certainly the incessant tail wagging is not possible with an undocked tail. The tail is set on just below the level of the back, and should not rise above the level of the back. This would constitute a 'gay' tail, which is an ugly fault. The nervous Cocker will move with its tail firmly clamped down and this, too, is a serious fault.

A dog's movement will often tell you how soundly he is put together. The judge will generally assess gait from the front, in profile, and from the rear.

GAIT AND MOVEMENT

The long, ground-covering stride is a result of good conformation combined with development. A long stride is more economical than a short, stepping movement. Sound movement is essential; the dog moving with parallel strides of good length and the hocks with good width between them. The backline of the dog should remain level.

COAT

The texture is important and the natural, well-prepared coat will remain flat and silky. Puppy coat is often woolly and profuse; with regular grooming this changes when the Cocker is about ten months old. The blacks and reds often carry very profuse, woolly puppy coats on their legs. In general, the solid colours do tend to carry heavier coats than the particolours.

The frequent use of thinning scissors, electric clippers and trimming knives alters the texture of the coat and the silkiness is lost, hence the advantage of finger-and-thumb trimming or hand-stripping, which is described later.

The Cocker Spaniel is distinguished by its wide range of colours.

COLOUR

One of the many attractions of the Cocker is its range of colours. The solid colours are represented by black, golden, red, black and tan, and liver – but the solid liver is something of a rarity today, as is the liver and tan combination.

The particolours range through black and white, orange and white, blue roans, orange roans, liver roans and tricolours such as black/white/tan, blue roan and tan.

SIZE

The Standard underlines the difference between the dog and the bitch. It should be easy to differentiate between them; the dog being a wider, heavier and more substantial specimen.

RING PROCEDURE

On the day of the show, arrive in good time. If the show is benched, then put your dog in his benching compartment and let him settle in. Before judging, you will need to brush and comb him – a grooming spray might be used to give extra gloss.

When your class is called, the ring steward will give out your ring number, published in the show catalogue, and you should pin this to your jacket. Then, you should set your dog up in the show position for the judge's first appraisal.

The judge will usually walk along the line of exhibits, taking his first impressions, and he will request that the dogs are moved

The judge will assess each dog individually, and will then evaluate the class.

around the ring. The dogs will be examined individually, on the table – your ringcraft lessons will have prepared you – and the dog will be moved, usually in a triangle, to assess his profile and his front and rear movement. After all the dogs have been examined in this way, the judge will come to his decision and call the winners into the centre of the ring.

If there is more than one class for Cockers, the first prize winners compete to decide the Best of Breed winner. Win or lose, you should regard showing as an enjoyable pastime. The judge's decision is final, and it is also one person's subjective opinion. You entered for a judge's opinion, and you must accept it. There will be another day, another judge and another opinion.

We take our dogs home and think them special. Competition in the Cocker Spaniel ring is tough and, if you are fortunate enough to receive a prize card, it is a great thrill. Showing Cockers regularly demands a lot of work and patience, and frequent disappointments. If you are highly competitive and find defeat difficult, then it would be better to avoid showing; enjoy your Cocker as a handsome and pleasure-giving family pet.

PRESENTATION

The coat, presentation, grooming and trimming of the dog are very important; you cannot expect to win top awards with an untidily presented dog. Such is the competition that you would have little chance. If you are going to show your dog regularly, then it is essential that you master the art of trimming for yourself. This way, you can keep your dog in good trim by working on him weekly, and about half an hour each week will keep him in shape. A local breeder of Cockers might be willing to show you how to trim, and then you must practise. If you plan only to show on a one-off occasion, a local exhibitor might be persuaded to trim your dog for the show. The chapter on trimming and grooming should help you.

The winner on the day – but win or lose – your dog is always special.

6 Breeding Cockers

The appeal of a litter of Cocker Spaniel puppies – playful, giving hours of pleasure – is understandable, but behind that picture lies a host of other issues; hours of hard work, responsibility for selling them to good homes, hereditary problems. So, before thinking about breeding from your bitch, consider these important matters.

POPULAR MYTHS

"It is natural for a bitch to bear pups." In the wild, yes, but we now live in a world of domesticated pets, with too many dogs of all breeds and cross-breeds being born. Thousands of homeless dogs are destroyed every year; thousands more are in the pounds of breed rescue schemes and welfare organisations. It is not always easy to sell pups, and finding suitable homes, where the dogs will be looked after for life, is a great responsibility. Too many

are sold to families as a child's plaything, which is soon replaced by a new toy so the dog becomes an unwanted encumbrance.

"It is a good way of making money." It sounds attractive; four or five pups at several hundred pounds each. But do not forget the stud fee, vet's fees if anything goes wrong, rearing costs and advertising. Ask serious breeders how much money they make from litters and they will tell you quite honestly that they often end up in deficit!

If you are serious in wanting to keep a puppy from your bitch and are breeding primarily for yourself, and if you are prepared to undertake the responsibilities involved, then go ahead; but make a balanced, informed decision and plan the breeding very carefully.

WHEN TO BREED

Before considering breeding from your bitch, she should be a healthy, typical specimen of the breed, free from hereditary faults that could be passed on to her puppies. Above all, she should be of typical Cocker temperament. Dogs of nervous or aggressive temperaments should never be bred from.

It is inadvisable to breed from a Cocker before her second season, and I prefer to wait until the bitch is about two years old. Before this time, she is still growing up and maturing herself.

HEREDITARY PROBLEMS

The Cocker, like most dogs, is susceptible to some hereditary problems. You should do all you can to research your bitch's background to see that there is no incidence of these (See Chapter Seven). Good temperament is paramount in any dog who is to be a family pet. The Cocker has built up a reputation over many years as the most loving, trustworthy, happy breed, and long may this continue. Your bitch and the stud dog you use should be absolutely typical, dependable, merry Cockers, before you even considering breeding.

CHOOSING A STUD DOG

You might have met another local Cocker during your walks, and be thinking how convenient it might be to use him as a mate for your bitch. This is the worst possible reason for choosing him. Mating, natural though it might be, is often a difficult exercise, and requires skilled human supervision. Besides, the pedigree and background of the male might be quite unsuitable for your bitch.

Also avoid the pet owner who advertises in your local newspaper. These are often people out to make money with no knowledge about breeding, pedigrees or the background of the dog. Consult a local breeder or exhibitor; these people are usually quite happy to give help and advice, even if it is to tell you not to breed, or that your bitch is not good enough to breed from. On the other hand, they might have a suitable stud dog themselves, or be able to inform you of another breeder who could help you.

If your bitch is a solid colour then you should use a dog of the same colour or colours. A particolour bitch should be bred with a particolour dog. Mixing solid with particolours in a breeding programme often produces unattractively marked puppies.

When you find a potential stud dog, find out all you can about him and his pedigree. He should be a good specimen of the breed, preferably a prize-winner, free from hereditary medical conditions and of the same Cocker temperament. He should also complement your bitch in his physical characteristics. You should be trying, even as a pet breeder, to improve on your bitch by choosing a dog who will improve the areas in which she falls short. So, ask the breeder or stud dog owner for their advice.

The stud dog you choose must be sound in mind and body, and a typical specimen of the breed.

PEDIGREE

Pedigree is important – it is your dog's family tree. A long pedigree in itself is valueless – every mongrel on the street has one! It is the quality of dogs on the pedigree which is important. You should perpetuate this by choosing a well-bred dog whose pedigree complements that of your bitch. In choosing a mate, there are three types of combination to consider.

LINE BREEDING is the mating together of distantly-related dog and bitch, who share a common ancestor in their pedigree. Many successful breeders use this method as a means of retaining breed type and quality in their stock. It is important, however, that the common ancestor is a sound-quality dog so that you are 'doubling-up' on his blood and type.

IN-BREEDING is the mating of closely-related stock such as brother to sister, father to daughter. Some breeders occasionally use this programme, but it is not recommended for the casual breeder who does not know the breed or the bloodlines and background in great depth.

OUTCROSSING is the mating of unrelated stock. Again, the

The aim of a breeding programme is to produce quality dogs of similar type.

background of the dog should contain quality dogs free from hereditary problems.

MATING

If you decide to go ahead with breeding from your bitch, consider the time of year when she will whelp (give birth). The gestation period is 63 days. Will the pups be born at a convenient time? Is it a holiday period, when nobody will want to be buying a puppy? Will it be near Christmas, when there is a danger of puppy sales which are unwanted soon after the festive season?

When your bitch comes into season and you see the first signs of bleeding, contact the owner of the stud dog. He will then calculate whether the dog is available on the appropriate day. Bitches vary as to the best day for mating, but, as a general rule, they are fertile when their discharge changes from blood-colour to a colourless, clear discharge, usually on the 12th or 13th day of the season. Your bitch will usually tell you when she is ready for mating with her flirtatious mating antics, swinging her tail to the side when touched on the hindquarters.

The mating itself needs skilled supervision, and an experienced stud dog owner will often prefer you to leave the proceedings entirely to him. Otherwise, you might be requested to hold the bitch quietly and reassuringly. Maiden bitches and pet bitches are sometimes a little nervous during the initial proceedings, and, to the uninitiated pet owner, the proceedings can be distasteful, and more than once I have removed a hysterical and doting pet owner from the room, and their bitch has then settled quite happily to be mated.

Usually one mating is sufficient if the bitch is fertile. Some breeders prefer to have a second mating after 36-48 hours. The stud fee should be paid at the time of mating, and the stud dog owner should provide you with a signed Kennel Club form, which gives the dog's KC name and registration number. These are essential for registering the resulting puppies. The owner should also provide you with the pedigree of the stud dog.

Most stud owners offer their dog on the basis of a free return mating if the bitch does not have puppies. Never use a dog who is not registered at the Kennel Club – this makes registering puppies impossible, and, in many people's eyes, reduces the value of the puppies. After mating, the bitch should be kept away from male dogs until her season is finished.

PREGNANCY

For the first few weeks, there will be no physical change in your bitch. The first sign is often a change in temperament, your Cocker becoming even more loving and a little more placid. By about the fifth week of pregnancy, there might be a thickening of the loins and the bitch's teats may become pink and upstanding. From the sixth week, the bitch's body will become noticeably bigger, and you can be fairly sure with these signs that she is in whelp. You may wish to seek your vet's opinion if you are unsure, or it is possible to have your bitch scanned, which will tell you not only if she is pregnant but can also tell how many puppies she is likely to have. I prefer to let nature take its course.

CARE OF THE BITCH IN WHELP

For the first few weeks, there will be no need to change your bitch's usual routine in feeding or exercise. She should be fit, not fat. Once you are sure she is in whelp, you can give her an extra meal each day; in the later stages, divide the amount into smaller meals in case she is uncomfortable after eating.

PREPARATION FOR WHELPING

As the time for whelping draws near, you should be prepared for the event. Decide where your bitch will whelp – it should be a quiet, warm room, and she should have a large whelping box, positioned clear of draughts. Later on, you may wish to place a play pen around this area to contain the puppies. Move the bitch into her whelping quarters a week or so before she is due to whelp so that she can settle into her maternity quarters. Save all your newspapers for lining the whelping box and as absorbent floor covering for the puppy pen.

Warmth is important. Cold can kill puppies, and, if conditions are cold, you should provide heating in some form, such as a heat light, a dull emitter lamp or a radiator in the room.

WHELPING

Many breeds will take the entire 63-day gestation period; some may go over by a day or so. Others, especially maiden bitches or those with large litters, will whelp early. The first signs are the bitch refusing her food for a day and becoming increasingly restless. Then, she will start scratching in the box or at the carpet, nature's

In most cases, whelping is a straightforward business, and the Cocker Spaniel bitch will be a caring mother.

equivalent of making her nest. This might last for a whole day before the bitch goes into the final stages of labour.

After the initial, unsettled period, the bitch should start to experience heavy contractions as she pushes the puppies along the neck of the uterus towards delivery. These muscular contractions, very noticeable and often accompanied by a groan or whimper, lead to the expulsion of the puppy. Before the first puppy arrives, the bitch should expel the water bag (the waters breaking), and, soon after this, the first puppy should be born. If heavy contractions persist for more than one hour and no puppy appears, consult your vet.

Puppies are usually born head first, and are delivered in a mucous sac full of amniotic fluid with the umbilical cord attached. Many bitches will break the sac open and bite the cord themselves, but you should be on hand and be prepared to do this if necessary. The umbilical cord should be severed about one inch from the puppy's abdomen; you can use sterilised scissors or your sterilised fingers. The puppy should be checked to ensure that his nose, mouth and throat are clear of mucus and fluid, and you can do this by gripping the puppy's body firmly, head down, and shaking him in a pendulum-like action to eject any remaining fluid. Then rub the puppy with a warm, rough towel, to dry him off and to stimulate breathing. Puppies that have been a long time in delivery often take a minute or so to recover. Shake, rub firmly and massage, and then the glorious moment of his first squeak, and you have your first live puppy.

With luck, the rest of the puppies will follow in a similar manner, with a period of rest

At eight days old, these puppies will spend all their time eating and sleeping.

before contractions restart. Let the bitch see her puppies; they are often ready to go straight on to the teat for a feed, but once contractions restart, place the puppies in a warm, towel-lined box, where the bitch can see them but out of danger of being damaged in the next delivery. Each puppy should be followed by an afterbirth, which the bitch might eat. If she does not, you should remove it.

COMPLICATIONS

You may encounter breech births, that is, the puppy is born feet first, and sometimes these are more difficult to deliver. Sometimes, puppies may get lodged in the vulva and cause the bitch (and you!) distress. In cases like this, you may help the bitch by lubricating your hand with a sterile jelly and trying to grip the puppy. As the bitch contracts and pushes, you should pull the puppy in a steady downward motion to help the bitch expel it. If you cannot free the pup, call the vet.

If the bitch goes into contractions and does not expel a puppy, consult your vet as she may be suffering from uterine inertia, and may need an injection to bring on the birth, or, in some cases, a Caesarean section may be required.

AFTER WHELPING

Once the puppies are delivered, it is essential that you give the bitch some peace and quiet to recover from her exertions and settle with the pups. Fluids are important for milk production, so offer her a drink of water with glucose, or a little milk and glucose. I am a great believer in honey as a natural food, and often put a teaspoonful of honey in fluids for the bitch. You may also allow the bitch out to relieve herself, and then give her time to settle. Ensure that all the puppies are suckling well. I usually pop in to see a nursing bitch every few hours to check that all is well.

COMPLICATIONS AFTER WHELPING

Unfortunately, there are a few problems which can occur, and you should be aware of these and keep your eyes open for any danger signals. You should check your pups for cleft palates and hare-lips which prevent them from feeding. These puppies should be taken to the vet for painless destruction.

You should check your bitch's

teats daily to ensure that she does not develop mastitis – a painful hardening of the teats which causes a milk blockage. A more serious problem is the occurrence of eclampsia (milk fever), which is caused by calcium deficiency in the bitch and produces the dramatic symptoms of quivering, nausea and occasional fits, and can result in death. If you notice any strange behaviour in the bitch, you should get her to the vet immediately, warning them of your arrival. She will need an intravenous injection of calcium to recover, and then the pups must be taken from her and reared by hand.

DEWCLAWS AND DOCKING

Puppies should have their dewclaws removed to prevent potential problems later through in-curling growth. Your vet will perform this simple operation, not requiring anaesthetic, at four days old. More problematic is the question of docking, the shortening of the Cocker's tail, as is traditional.

Recent criticism from animal welfare societies has meant that it is now illegal for breeders to dock their puppies' tails as they often did, and must leave the operation to be performed by a vet. However, as most of the veterinary profession are opposed to docking, regarding it as a cosmetic operation, it can be difficult to find a vet to perform the operation.

The reasons for the docking tradition are rooted in the working function of the Cocker, and allied to its incessant tail action. Left at full length, the tail is susceptible to injury, and often requires amputation. This is why the docking tradition has been maintained, despite the fact that not many Cockers are used for gundog work today. However, for many, myself included, the docked tail is a feature of Cocker breed type, and I would be unhappy to see a total ban. The docking operation takes only a second, causing little distress, and the puppies are back suckling with their mothers immediately.

However, it is for you to decide whether you wish your litter to be docked or not. If you decide on docking and your own vet is unwilling to perform the operation, you could consult local Cocker breeders, who will probably know of a vet who will dock. Owners in the UK could also write to the Council for

Docked Breeds, an organisation dedicated to retaining the right to dock traditionally-docked breeds.

REARING

For the first three or four weeks, a healthy bitch with plenty of milk should be quite capable of feeding an average-sized litter. Of course, she must be very well fed with three or four high-protein meals a day, and I like to feed extra calcium and mineral supplements during this period, which can be very draining on the bitch's natural resources. Most Cockers make excellent mothers, and are content to stay in the whelping box all day, sometimes unwilling to come out even for calls of nature. These early weeks should be a pleasurable time for you and the bitch. Keep your eye on the bitch and pups, ensure that all are getting fed and growing fatter but, apart from that, give the bitch plenty of time and peace to enjoy motherhood. Besides, you need to store up your energy for the hard work which is coming in the following weeks of rearing the litter!

WEANING

At four weeks, your Cocker puppies will be waddling about their box. Their mother might be getting a little bored with them, and her milk supply will be now insufficient to feed the growing pups. This is the time to start weaning the pups from their mother and introducing them to semi-solid and solid food.

I start my pups on Farley's Rusks or Farex soaked in warm milk, with a little honey added. I mix this into a thick paste and offer a shallow dish to the pups, introducing them individually, and often tempting them with a fingertip covered with the paste, gradually coaxing them towards the dish. Ensure that each individual can lap, and then, depending on the size of the litter, let them share the dish or divide into several dishes so that every pup can feed.

The first attempts are usually messy and chaotic, with paste-covered faces, pups falling into the bowl and paddling around in the contents. Keep plenty of kitchen rolls handy for mopping-up operations, and now is the time to use all your old newspapers for covering the floor of your puppy area.

After the initial introduction to semi-solid food, you might introduce the pup to rice pudding,

Weaning can be started from around four weeks of age, and, in no time, the litter will be tucking into solid food.

breakfast cereal biscuits and milk or scrambled eggs. From here, you can advance to solid food. I have found that finely-scraped and minced beef, chicken, or carefully-boned and mashed pilchards are irresistible to most puppies. You can mix these with a little crumbled breakfast cereal biscuit and, later, the smallest puppy meal, which I soak in hot water or gravy and allow to crumble and go cool.

You can now buy complete puppy weaning preparations, which provide a nutritionally-balanced food, often requiring just soaking in water. Many breeders have found these excellent. I have nothing against these products, but I prefer to give my pups variety to prepare them for their new homes. I also provide a diet sheet for the puppies' new owners.

Make sure fresh drinking water is available in a non-tip bowl.

The weaning process is a gradual one, and, even when the pups are accepting semi-solid and solid food, they should still have the opportunity to feed from their mother. She will still be producing milk, albeit less of it, and this needs to be used. Besides, it is the most natural food for the pups, and it is free.

Once you have started feeding the pups, give them one or two meals a day, and let them take the rest of their nourishment from their mother. By six weeks of age, they should be almost completely weaned, and visiting their mother only occasionally. Mother, by this time, will probably be quite happy to leave the pups and return to her family life – jumping in to see her pups for short spells. Remember

A job well done – two eight-week-old pups ready to go to their new homes.

also to trim the sharp edges off the puppies' nails – sharp nails can cause the bitch much pain when her pups are feeding from her.

WORMING

Some puppies will have ringworm infestation and it is essential that you worm the litter at about five weeks of age, and, perhaps, if the infestation is heavy, once more before parting with the litter. There are many preparations on the market, but I suggest that you ask your vet for his recommendation for the puppies and their mother.

SELLING YOUR PUPPIES

Many owners find it very difficult to part with their puppies; others are so exhausted from all the work involved that they are relieved when life can return to normal. If you have to advertise your pups, you may choose to advertise in the local newspaper, or you could use one of the national canine journals. When prospective purchasers come to view the puppies, you should vet them to ensure that they would make suitable owners who are going to give your puppy a good home life. Homes where a puppy will be left alone all day are not suitable – it is a lonely life, and puppies become unhappy, bored and destructive. Homes where puppies are to be a toy for young children are also a bad idea. Children are often unaware of the needs of a puppy or the responsibilities involved.

On the other hand, I have met some delightful people through selling puppies to them, people who have become friends of many years' standing. There is nothing nicer than to receive Christmas cards and photographs of much-loved family pets, and, years later, the same people ring up to tell me of their sadness at losing their pet and their desire to replace him with another. These are the sort of things that make dog breeding a pleasure.

7 Health Care

Your Cocker's happiness and health are your responsibility, and the first steps are through good feeding, regular exercise and regular grooming. With ordinary luck and good husbandry, your Cocker will remain healthy and happy for many years.

INOCULATIONS

As we would do with our human babies, we inoculate our puppies to protect them against the life-threatening canine diseases. It is essential that you take your puppy at around ten weeks of age to be inoculated against distemper, hardpad, leptospirosis, hepatitis and parvovirus. After the first injection, you will need to return a fortnight later for the completion of the course, and you should then keep your Cocker on your own property for two weeks. After this time you can take him out into the wide world. You will be provided with a certificate of inoculation and required to return regularly for booster injections, especially if you wish to put your pet into boarding kennels at any time, as no reputable boarding kennel will accept your pet without proof of inoculation.

WORMING

When you take your puppy for his inoculation, the vet will usually give your pup a routine health check. Ask at this time for his recommendation for future worming, which should be a routine practice each year, or when you suspect your Cocker has a worm infestation. Signs of infestation are loss of condition, a dry coat, bad breath and a voracious appetite. It is also sometimes signalled by your dog pulling himself along the ground on his backside.

After worming, your puppy may expel visible worms in his motions, but many treatments

The vet will give your puppy a routine health check when you start his inoculation programme.

dissolve the worms before expulsion. Take great care removing and disposing of the waste.

ANAL GLANDS

Distasteful though the subject might be, blockage of the anal glands is quite common in all dogs, and is caused by a build-up of mucus in the glands, which are located on either side of the anus. Symptoms include the dog dragging himself along the floor on his backside or a swelling around the anus. The treatment is extremely easy, and you can visit your vet, or, much less expensively, do it yourself.

While somebody holds the dog's head, place a thick wad of warm, moist kitchen tissue on the dog's anal area, and exert pressure with your thumbs on either side of the anus. This should expel the mucus into the wad, and the problem is solved. If you are unsuccessful in your attempt, take your dog to the vet and watch how it is done.

FLEAS

Flea infestations are a fairly common occurrence in long-coated dogs, but, through regular grooming and good husbandry, you can minimise the chances of infestation. Fleas are minute and hard to see. When you groom your Cocker, you may notice the dark droppings of fleas which have been feeding off your pet. Fleas do not necessarily live on your pet, but can live in any warm place, such as carpets and dog blankets. They will often secrete themselves in the warmest parts of the dog: behind the ears, under the elbows or in thick coat, and will cause your dog to itch and scratch. There are many good preparations available for the quick eradication of fleas. Consult your vet. Follow the instructions and spray the dog's sleeping quarters at the same time as you treat the dog.

LICE

Lice are small, brownish or white insects which breed on the dog and, like fleas, enjoy warm places. You can, again, purchase an insecticide spray or a preparation for bathing your dog. Make sure you follow the maker's recommendations and instructions when using these products.

TICKS

These are blood-sucking mites which bury their teeth in the dog's skin, grip to them and grow fatter as they suck blood. They can cause irritation and skin infections. They are usually picked up by the dog running though grass or moorland, especially if it is in sheep territory. You can remove these ticks by applying a swab soaked in surgical spirit to them. This loosens the grip of the tick, and you can then carefully pull the tick out using tweezers. Some insecticidal shampoos also help prevent infestation.

UPSET STOMACH

Cockers are usually very good eaters, always ready to eat and still looking appealingly at any food in the area for second helpings. Overeating is only one of the possible causes of sickness and diarrhoea. If your Cocker is sick and suffers from diarrhoea but has no other symptoms of illness, starve him for 24 hours, allowing access to water only. If the condition improves, then you can introduce light food such as chicken or fish and rice for a couple of days, before reverting to the usual diet. If vomiting and diarrhoea persist after 24 hours' fasting, then you should take your Cocker to the vet.

INTERDIGITAL CYSTS

These are painful blisters which

form between the toes, and can first be diagnosed by the dog licking his feet. I have found that dogs exercised on the beach are particularly prone to these cysts, although they can also be caused by grass seeds and other foreign bodies becoming lodged between the toes. You can relieve these sores through bathing in a solution of antiseptic lotion and water, or a saline solution. Fill a jam jar or pot with the solution, and place the affected foot in the pot and allow it to soak. Then dry with tissue. I have found that disinfectant cream can help, but in extreme cases the condition may need veterinary treatment.

POISONING

In this age of chemicals and insecticides being used more widely, there is a risk that your dog could come into contact with a toxic substance, and the effect can be dramatic and fatal.

Signs to look out for are vomiting, a craving to drink heavily, and complete collapse. Check the gums – they can lose all colour and become anaemic or jaundiced. In cases of suspected poisoning, it is vital that you get

your dog to the vet immediately, having warned them that you are on the way with an urgent case. If you have a garden, you must be very careful that any fertilisers, weedkillers or garden preparations you might use are safe for animals.

INHERITED CONDITIONS

All pedigree dogs may inherit certain diseases and conditions, and although the Cocker Spaniel has few such problems, it is sensible to be aware of breed specific problems.

PROGRESSIVE RETINAL ATROPHY (PRA): This is a hereditary eye condition often known as night-blindness. You should have your bitch checked for this condition, and use a stud dog who is also unaffected.

HIP DYSPLASIA (HD): This is a condition affecting the hindlegs of the dog, and can result in painful lameness at an early age. Although there have not been many published cases of HD in this country, some breeders are having their dogs X-rayed for this condition.

FAMILIAL NEPHRITIS (FN): A few years ago, there was a disturbing number of young Cockers dying from a debilitating illness, where they lost weight rapidly and would not respond to any treatment. Post-mortem examinations revealed a form of kidney failure through shrunken kidneys. This was more prevalent in the particolour Cockers, but, through the diligence and testing of breeders, this has, thankfully, diminished and is nowadays very rare.

RAGE SYNDROME: This title was given to the condition of aggressive, unreliable temperament in some Cockers, who would suddenly change character and become attacking, vicious biters. They were found more predominantly in the red Cocker, and, again, breeders have recorded the background of dogs exhibiting these symptoms. Fortunately, these cases are rare, and breeders have been assiduous in avoiding suspect bloodlines.

THE ELDERLY COCKER

Many Cockers will live to 12 years of age or more and remain fit and healthy. As the dog gets older, he will require less exercise and be happy with shorter walks, or just content in the garden.

Accordingly, he will need a little less food to prevent obesity. Some geriatric dogs do lose body weight, and then you can increase the food. Dogs of all breeds seem to develop more character as they get older, and Cockers are no exception; lovely to look at, full of devotion and with an irresistible expression. Keep him warm at night, well-fed, regularly groomed and his old age need not be troublesome.

EUTHANASIA

There comes a time when we must face saying goodbye to our faithful and much-loved Cocker Spaniel, who has been a member of the family through ups and downs and has always been a source of comfort and pleasure. When a geriatric dog begins to fail in health and his quality of life declines so much that life is painful or no longer a pleasure, it is the least we can do to put him out of discomfort. Painless euthanasia involves the injection of a large dose of anaesthetic, and the dog will drift off quickly and painlessly. I know it is distressing for loving owners, but stay with your pet, reassure him and say your last goodbye. If you have the space and facilities, you may wish to inter your pet in the garden. Alternatively, most veterinary practices offer a cremation service.

Your home will feel empty and sad without your Cocker's presence. Whether you replace him or not is a personal matter – you may feel a sense of disloyalty if you thought about having another Cocker, or you could view it as a compliment to your last pet. Whatever course you take, give thanks for the pleasure and the joy that you have had by sharing a period of your life with a merry Cocker.